6:00 p.m.

Houses begin to collapse under the weight of the falling ash and pumice.

25 August, 6:30 a.m.

The ash cloud begins to surge down the mountainside and crashes into Pompeii. Two thousand people are suffocated and buried beneath the red-hot volcanic debris.

11:00 p.m.

Earthquakes shake the region throughout the night.

1:00 p.m.

The air is choked with ash. Vesuvius explodes and an enormous ash cloud rises into the sky.

AD 1748

Treasure-hunters begin the first of many excavations at Pompeii.

Map of Pompeii and Campania

Pompeii is in the region of Campania, a hilly and mountainous area of southern Italy. It is one of many towns along the coast, and is one of the closest to Mount Vesuvius, the region's highest hill.

In the centuries leading up to the famous volcanic eruption, the region had been dominated by the city of Capua after its founding in the 8th century BC. This city was fought over by the Carthaginian general Hannibal and the Romans during the Second Punic War from 216–211 BC, before eventually becoming allied with the Romans.

The area was completely Romanized by the 1st century BC, and became a wealthy part of the Roman Empire.

Timeline of Pompeii

AD 62

The region surrounding Pompeii is damaged by an earthquake.

August, AD 79

The crops in the mountain vineyards mysteriously wither and die. Gas that smells like rotten eggs leaks from the ground.

24 August, AD 79, 10:00 a.m.

A series of small explosions is followed by smoke rising from Vesuvius and a light rain of ash.

AD 79

The damage caused by the earthquake has been mostly repaired and life has returned to normal.

20 August, AD 79

The first tremors are felt in Pompeii.

Author:

John Malam studied ancient history and archaeology at the University of Birmingham, England, after which he worked as an archaeologist at the Ironbridge Gorge Museum, in Shropshire, England. He is now an author, specialising in information books for children. He lives in Cheshire with his wife, a book designer, and their two children.

Artist:

David Antram was born in Brighton, England, in 1958. He studied at Eastbourne College of Art and then worked in advertising for 15 years before becoming a full-time artist. He has illustrated many children's nonfiction books.

Series Creator:

David Salariya was born in Dundee, Scotland. He has illustrated a wide range of books and has created and designed many new series for publishers both in the UK and overseas. In 1989, he established The Salariya Book Company. He lives in Brighton with his wife, illustrator Shirley Willis, and their son, Jonathan.

Editor: **Sophie Izod**

Published in Great Britain in MMXVIII by Book House, an imprint of
The Salariya Book Company Ltd
25 Marlborough Place, Brighton BN1 1UB
www.salariya.com

ISBN: 978-1-912233-45-8

1 3 5 7 9 8 6 4 2

A CIP catalogue record for this book is available from the British Library.
Printed and bound in China.

Visit
www.salariya.com
for our online catalogue and **free** fun stuff.

PAPER FROM
SUSTAINABLE
FORESTS

You Wouldn't Want to Live in Pompeii! ™

Written by
John Malam

Illustrated by
David Antram

Created and designed by
David Salariya

A Volcanic Eruption You'd Rather Avoid

BOOK HOUSE
a SALARIYA *imprint*

Contents

Introduction

The year is AD 79, and you are in Pompeii, a small, pleasant Roman town in the south of Italy. You've spent most of your life here, but Pompeii isn't your home town. You were born in Greece, and Greek is your first language. As a young man you were taught to read and write in Greek, and you learned about the poets, writers and thinkers of Greece. You had dreams of becoming one of them yourself.

But you were captured by pirates, who sold you to a slave dealer. You became the property of a wealthy Roman family. You've been with them so long, you're one of the family now, but don't get any ideas – you're still a slave! Now, as an older man, you've become a paedagogus – a slave who looks after your master's son at home and at school. You're his buddy, whether he likes it or not.

The long, hot summer of AD 79 starts like all those that have gone before it – but soon you will wish you were anywhere but in Pompeii!

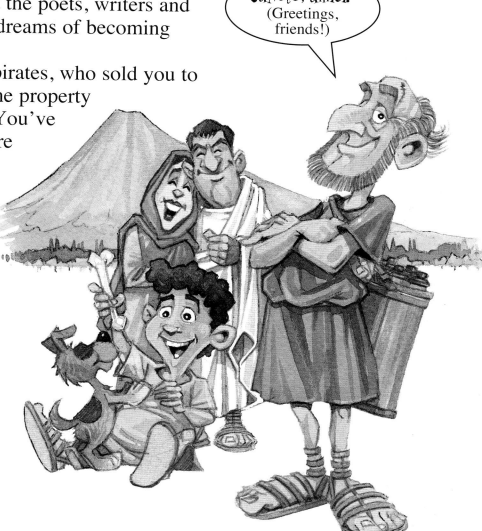

Salvete, amici!*
(Greetings, friends!)

*Latin is the language of the Roman Empire.

9

Earthquake! Flashback to AD 62

Damage across the region

HERCULANEUM. This nearby town suffered major damage to its public buildings, and people were very frightened.

NEAPOLIS. Less damage was caused here, as the town was further from the centre of the quake.

ANIMALS. A flock of 600 sheep dropped dead of shock near Pompeii.

STATUES. As the ground shook, statues wobbled until they cracked and fell.

A good slave works hard, doesn't complain, and doesn't run away. Most of all, a slave should be loyal, obedient and trustworthy. You proved how useful you were when you saved your owners' lives. It was 17 years ago, when an earthquake rocked Pompeii and the surrounding countryside. As buildings fell, you led your master and mistress to safety. You put their lives before your own, and almost died when a roof tile hit your head. That tremor was a warning sign from Vesuvius. The hill was slowly waking from its long sleep – but no-one realised this at the time.

Quid est?
(What is it?)

5 February AD 62

Ecce signum!
(Look, a sign!)

EMPEROR SURVIVES EARTHQUAKE.
In AD 64 there was another earthquake. Emperor Nero was in Neapolis, acting in a play. He was unharmed, and took this as a sign that the gods were protecting him.

SLEEPING GIANT. Close to Pompeii is Mount Vesuvius. Some say that it poured forth monstrous fire in ancient times, but it doesn't now.

Handy hint

Protect your master and mistress. Then they will be kind to you – they will not get rid of you.

Domine! Domina! Hac! Agite!
(Master! Mistress! This way! Come on!)

Fix it! Rebuilding Pompeii

The earthquake of AD 62 is now a distant memory. Today, in AD 79, life has returned to normal for the people of Pompeii. Most of the buildings damaged in the earthquake were repaired long ago, but in a few places builders are still at work even now.

Over the years, your owners have been good to you. When their son was born, they made you his paedagogus – his own personal slave. It's an important and responsible job. An educated Greek like you makes the best companion for the son of a wealthy Roman. You must teach him your wisdom and knowledge.

EARTHQUAKE PICTURE. This carving in stone shows buildings damaged in the quake of AD 62.

MOSAIC PICTURE. *Tesserae* – tiny cubes of coloured stone – are used to make hard-wearing mosaic floors.

WALL PAINTING. An artist has painted a view of Vesuvius on the wall of a house.

20 August AD 79

The boy loves to hear the story of how you saved his parents from the earthquake – and each time you tell it, it gets better! Like the Greek storytellers of old, you go on and on, weaving an ever grander tale. You're even starting to believe it yourself!

Handy hint

Make toys for your master's son. If the boy likes them, your master will be pleased with you too.

Centum tegulae in caput meum caderunt!
(A hundred tiles fell on my head!)

Mendax!
(Liar!)

Impossibile!
(No way!)

Senex veterator!
(Old rogue!)

Mirabile!
(Cool!)

School! Looking after your master's son

It costs his parents eight asses a month to send him to school. Make sure it's money well spent.

Clap!

Animum adverte ad magistrum!
(Pay attention to the teacher!)

Long ago, the famous Greek philosopher Plato said: 'A sheep can no more live without a shepherd than a boy without a paedagogus.' And so it is: you are like a shepherd for your master's son. Without you to take him to school, and watch over him in lessons, he would be like a little lost lamb. You are his companion and friend; you are always there for him. At school, a *magister* (teacher) will teach him reading, writing, and possibly numbers, but you will give him his real education. You must prepare him for adult life, instructing him about the ways of the world, and how a good Roman should behave in public and in private. Tell him what is right and wrong, and what is good and bad. Do these things well, and your master can ask no more of you.

GET UP. Wake him at daybreak. Open the window to let light into his bedroom.

GET WASHED. Bring him a bowl of water so he can wash his face and hands.

GET DRESSED. Help him take off his nightshirt, then put on his tunic and sandals.

21 August AD 79

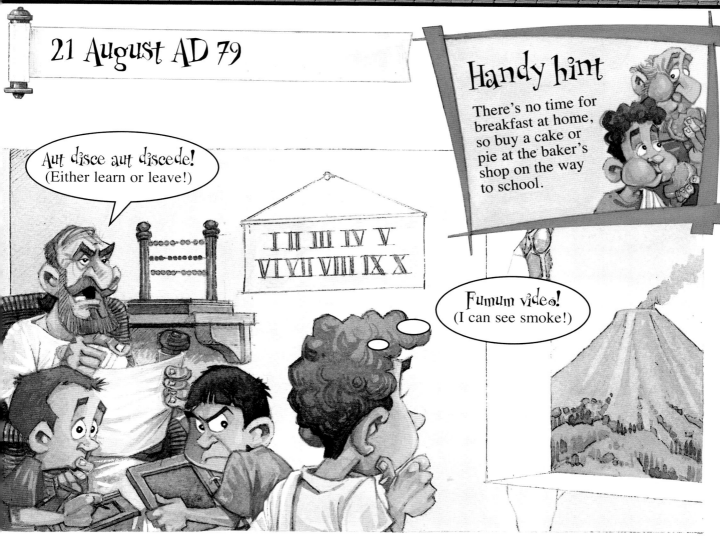

Aut disce aut discede!
(Either learn or leave!)

Fumum video!
(I can see smoke!)

Handy hint

There's no time for breakfast at home, so buy a cake or pie at the baker's shop on the way to school.

GET TIDY. Hand him a comb and make sure he uses it! His hair should be neat and tidy.

GET PACKED. You carry his inkstand, pens, books and writing tablets in a *scrinium*.

GET GOING. Then set off for the schoolroom. As a slave, you must walk behind the boy.

Day out! A visit to a vineyard

Your owner is a businessman. He plans to buy a large quantity of grapes from vineyards on the slopes of Mount Vesuvius, and turn them into red wine. He'll sell it in the markets of Pompeii, and make a lot of money. Vines grow well in the mountain's fertile soil, but this year the farmers are worried. They're saying that many vines are wilting and starting to die. Instead of swelling with juice, the grapes are shrivelling up and will be no good for wine. This news has troubled your owner, so he's gone to a vineyard to investigate, and he's taken you with him. The farmer doesn't know what's killing the vines – and he's even more puzzled by strange wisps of steam and smoke coming from the ground. They smell of rotten eggs!

Around Pompeii

THE RIVER. The Sarno links Pompeii to the sea, and waters the fields.

SEA SALT. At the coast, sea water is evaporated in shallow pools (salt pans) to leave salt crystals.

BIG HOUSES. The richest Romans have country villas, where they live in luxury.

OLIVE GROVES. Olive trees grow well here, and make the finest olive oil.

22 August AD 79

THE GOD'S OWN MOUNTAIN. Grapes grow so well here that Vesuvius is said to be the home of Bacchus, the god of wine.

GODS' GIFT. The first grapes of the year were picked on the 19th of August, and a lamb was sacrificed to the gods.

Handy hint

You'll be doing plenty of walking today. Instead of your usual sandals, wear lace-up walking boots.

Desiste! (Stop it!)

Nolo! Admodum ridiculum est! (No! It's a lot of fun!)

Sicut ova mala. (It's like bad eggs.)

Quod foetet? (What's that smell?)

WHEAT FIELDS. Farmers harvest wheat by hand. The grain makes flour for bread.

SHEEP FARMING. Sheep provide wool and sheepskins for clothing and bedding.

17

Gladiators! The games come to town

On the east side of Pompeii is the amphitheatre – a big open-air building where people watch gladiatorial games and animal fights. It's quite old-fashioned: it only has two entrances, and there's no machinery to move scenery around. Twenty years ago, in AD 59, there was a riot here when visitors from nearby Nuceria came to watch the games. They insulted the Pompeians, spat at them, and tossed seat cushions around. And when someone threw a stone at an official, the Pompeians had had enough. The crowd got onto the sand of the arena and fought like gladiators! Fighting spilled into the streets, and many were killed. After that, all games were banned at Pompeii for ten years. Enjoy today's show, but keep out of trouble!

Look out for:

NOTICES. You'll know when the games are coming because painted signs will appear on buildings, with dates and times.

Age! (Go for it!)

Referee

Charon

Volcano,* optimo, maximo! (To Vulcan, the best, the greatest!)

*Yes, the modern word *volcano* comes from the name of the Roman god of fire.

FESTIVAL OF VULCAN. Today, the 23rd of August, is the annual festival of Vulcan, god of fire. Watch as priests sacrifice fish and sheep to Vulcan, and ask him to protect Pompeii and its people.

The man dressed as Charon (the ferryman of the underworld) hits the defeated gladiators with his mallet.

23 August AD 79

GRAFFITI. Fans put names and pictures of their favourite gladiators on walls. It shows who they support.

Handy hint

Don't upset the Nucerians! They're still annoyed about losing the riot, and they'd love to get even with you!

Abeo!
(I'm outta here!)

Mitte!
(Let him go!)

Iugula!
(Kill him!)

STREET MARKET. Traders set up stalls outside the arena. Buy bread, cheese, pies, fish sauce** and fruit, which you can eat as you watch the games.

Perfac diem meum!
(Make my day!)

**Very popular! But you wouldn't want to live near the place where they make it.

19

Little bang! Vesuvius wakes up

The summer of AD 79 has been strangely different from other summers. This year you've noticed many odd things, from dead fish floating in the river to smelly gas escaping from the ground. Are these signs of something bad about to happen? People carry on as normal, but they feel uneasy.

Today begins like any other. You take your master's son to school, and stay with him as he does his lessons. But when a series of small bangs are heard coming from Mount Vesuvius, you both go into the street to see what's happening. Rising from the summit is a dirty grey cloud, and a light rain of ash is falling from the sky. No doubt about it: something very strange is going on!

Warning signs

NOISES. With each tremor came a loud booming noise from under the ground.

DROUGHT. Wells and springs that should be full of fresh water have dried up.

TREMORS. The first shakes were felt about four days ago, on the 20th of August. They were quite strong, and cups and plates got broken.

FISH. The River Sarno is full of dead fish, as if it has been poisoned.

FUMES. Smoke and gas have started coming out of holes in the ground.

GRAPES. Grapes that should be ripe have withered on the vines.

Big bang! Vesuvius blows its top

People stare in wonder at the cloud rising from Mount Vesuvius. Some begin to panic and run for their lives – but you know that your duty is to stay with your young master. In fading light you make your way through the gloomy streets, taking him home to his parents – no more school for him today!

By midday the air is choked with ash, and day has turned to night. The volcano's gases stink of bad eggs, and it's getting harder to breathe. You think you will be safe in the house, but you soon realise you were wrong. In the early afternoon, an ear-bursting explosion rips the top off Vesuvius, and a huge cloud of dust and pumice rises into the sky.

Here's what's happened

1. MAGMA CHAMBER. A space underneath Mount Vesuvius has filled up with molten rock or *magma*. It's under great pressure.

2. MAGMA RISES. As the pressure increases, the magma is forced out of the chamber and up towards the surface along a *conduit* or pipe.

3. PUMICE. Near the top of the conduit, the red-hot magma cools and mixes with gases to make *pumice* – a lightweight rock filled with air bubbles.

4. EXPLOSION. A high-speed jet of gas rushes along the conduit and forces the pumice and tonnes of grey ash into the sky. Big bang!

24 August AD 79, 1:00 p.m.

Babae! (Wow!)

Terribile! (It's dreadful!)

Fugiendum est. (We'll have to go.)

Handy hint

Say your prayers! Go to the shrine of your household gods and pray that they will spare your life.

15km (9.3 miles)

5. ASH CLOUD. Because the gases are lighter than the surrounding air, they rise high into the sky, taking the ash with them.

6. WIND. The wind blows the ash cloud to the south-east, towards Pompeii. Ash falls from the cloud and settles on the town.

Vesuvius

Pompeii

5

6

Panic! Pompeii in chaos

Ash and pumice have been falling steadily for the last five hours. As the layer gets deeper, house roofs sag under the weight, and by late afternoon the first ones collapse. Fear grips the town, and people scramble to get out, along the road to Nuceria. They take their money and jewellery with them. Some try to take shelter in your house, but they're not welcome. The sound of pumice clattering onto the building is non-stop, and you have to shout to make yourself heard. Your master packs a chest with his family's most treasured possessions. Soon it will be time for you all to leave.

Adiuvate nos!
(Help us!)

REFUGEES. The people of Pompeii gather up their belongings and leave town.

LOOTERS. Some people seize the chance to steal from the empty houses.

WHITE TO GREY. As more pumice falls, it changes colour from white to grey.

1m
(3ft)

2.5m
(8ft)

24 August AD 79, 6:00 p.m.

Handy hint
Keep checking how deep the ash layer is – if it gets too deep you'll be trapped in the house.

UCH! Grey pumice is twice the size of the white, and hurts if it hits you.

COLLAPSE. From late afternoon roofs cave in under the weight of the pumice.

BLOCKED. Pumice floats, and it soon clogs up the River Sarno.

Run! It's time to leave

Terror on the streets

VOICES. It's now so dark that people cannot see their way. They call out for their loved ones.

Claudia!

Marce! (Marcus!)

Pater! (Dad!)

Mater! (Mum!)

DEAFENING NOISE. The rain of pumice gets stronger. As millions of pieces crash to the ground, it sounds like the roar of thunder.

It's been the worst day of your life, and it's not about to get any easier. Ash and pumice have been falling onto Pompeii for the last seven hours, and the town is slowly but surely being buried by the fallout from the volcano. Your master has finally decided to leave the house and try to lead his family to safety. But the door won't open, because there's so much ash and pumice stacked against it. You have to climb out through a window. It's soft underfoot, like gritty sand, and the weight of the family's treasure chest pulls you down. With every step you sink to your knees, and walking – or wading – gets harder. Your master and his son protect their heads from falling debris with cushions. The family stays together. They move faster than you, and very soon you are left alone in the choking, noisy darkness.

END OF THE WORLD? People think the world is coming to an end. Some say the gods have deserted them.

LAST GASP. The air is filled with poisonous fumes. People choke as they breathe. Ash and pumice threaten to bury them alive.

It's over! Well, that's what you think!

At the very end of this terrible day the hail of pumice slows down, and it's not as noisy as before. People who are still in Pompeii venture into the wrecked streets, and begin to wonder if the nightmare is coming to an end. (It's not. It's really only the quiet before the storm.)

You now feel totally abandoned, with only the family pet for company. As for your owners and their son, you pray to the gods that they found a way to get out of Pompeii, and are now safe from harm. Perhaps one day you will see them again.

As the long, dark hours of night slowly pass, you feel the ground shaking as earthquakes continue to rumble all around. From Vesuvius you hear a booming, roaring noise, as if something very heavy is rolling along the ground. It seems that Mount Vesuvius has not finished with Pompeii yet. What a miserable night!

Danger at sea

LAST SHIP. Your owners make it to the port, and catch the last ship to leave Pompeii. The harbour is full of pumice floating on the water, and the sea is rough.

GIANT WAVE. Late at night the sea is pulled back from the shore. It comes back as a tidal wave and smashes into the coast.

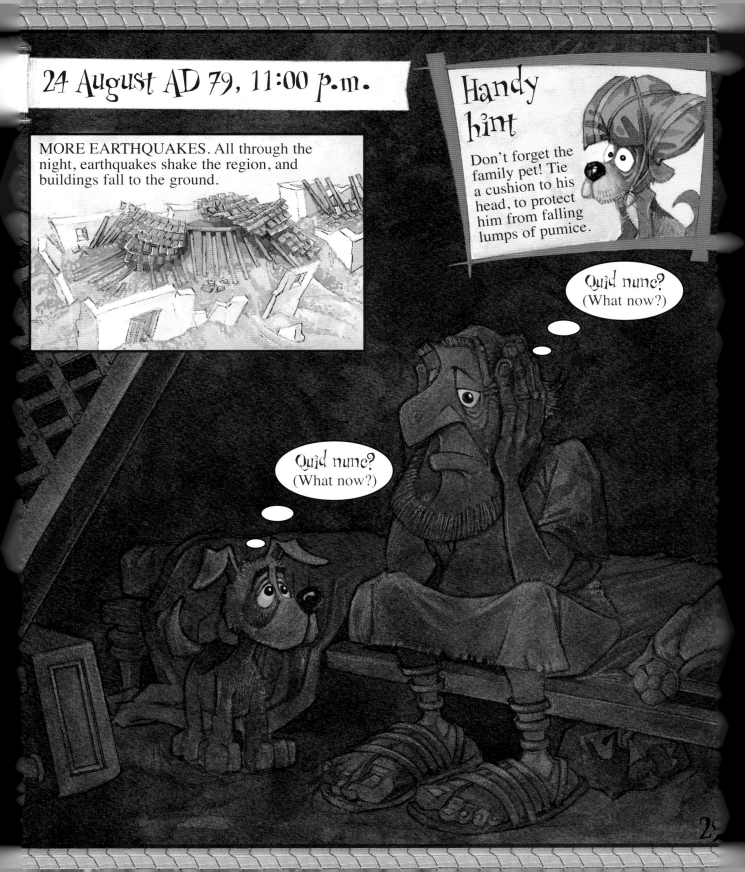

The end! Death of a town

The end comes suddenly. At half-past six on the morning of the 25th of August, the cloud of ash and pumice spewed out by Vesuvius begins to fall back to earth. Millions of tonnes of red-hot volcanic debris surge down the mountainside at great speed, reaching the town wall in minutes. Those caught by it are suffocated by the deadly fumes. More surges follow, blanketing the streets and buildings. It is all over in just thirty minutes. Pompeii, the town that 15,000 people had once called home, is buried beneath a deep layer of ash. Only the tops of the tallest buildings can be seen.

The last day of Pompeii

DAYBREAK. The fall of pumice slows right down. People make a last bid to flee from the town.

SULPHUR GAS. The choking smell of rotten eggs in the air increases, and it becomes even harder to breathe.

LIGHTNING. Bolts of lightning flash through the sky, and for a split second they light up what's left of Pompeii.

TOTAL DESTRUCTION. The first surge of boiling ash and pumice reaches the town walls. The next ones overwhelm the town.

Handy hint

There are plenty of horses on the loose. Grab one and hold on for dear life as it races to safety.

In the days and weeks that follow, survivors dig through the ash to recover statues of the gods. Emperor Titus visits the devastated area the following year. He orders repairs to some towns, but nothing is done for Pompeii. It is left as a graveyard for the 2,000 Pompeians who died in the eruption.

HEAD FOR NUCERIA. The ash and pumice are not so deep in that direction.

MISSING PERSONS. In Nuceria, you put up notices asking for information about your missing family.

Finis est omnium!
(It's the end of everything!)

HAPPY FAMILY! Your family hasn't forgotten you. Their ship took them to safety, but they never gave up hope of finding you alive. They saw your notices in Nuceria, and at last you are reunited with them.

Found! Pompeii uncovered
Dig, dig, dig

Pompeii was almost forgotten. Even its true name slipped from memory, and local people referred to it simply as 'la città', meaning 'the city'. The modern story of Pompeii begins in 1748, when treasure-hunters began the first of many excavations to find valuable objects. In 1763 a carved stone was found that gave the name of the town.

DIGGING BEGINS.
At first, people were only interested in finding statues and valuables.

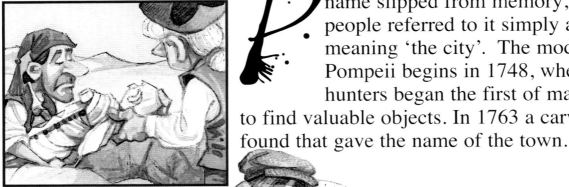

PLASTER CASTS.
In the 1860s, Giuseppe Fiorelli poured plaster into hollows in the ash, where bodies had been. It set hard, revealing the body shapes of long-dead Romans.

TOWN PLAN.
Most of Pompeii has now been uncovered.

Amphitheatre

Areas not yet excavated

32

Today, Pompeii is a Roman time capsule, and as visitors walk along the ancient streets and look into shops and houses, it's as if they have been transported back in time to August AD 79. But just north of the ruins is the sleeping Mount Vesuvius. It's a constant reminder of what destroyed Pompeii – and also preserved it for the future.

Handy hint

If you're one of the millions of people who live near Vesuvius today, watch the volcano closely – and hope it stays asleep!

...and found almost 2,000 years later!

Lost on the 24th of August AD 79...

ASLEEP AGAIN. Today, Mount Vesuvius is dormant. This means it is not erupting now, but is still capable of erupting. The latest eruption was in 1944.

Glossary

Amphitheatre An open-air building where gladiatorial contests and animal hunts were held.

Arena The floor of an amphitheatre. *Arena* is Latin for 'sand'.

As A Roman coin made from copper, and worth very little.

Bacchus The Roman god of wine.

Charon In Roman myth, the boatman who ferries souls to the underworld.

Dormant (Referring to a volcano) in a 'sleeping' phase, neither **active** (erupting from time to time) nor extinct.

Extinct (Referring to a volcano) having come to the end of its life, so that it will never erupt again.

Gladiator A person who has been trained to fight in the arena to entertain an audience. His main weapon is the **gladius** – a short stabbing sword.

Graffiti Words and pictures scratched or painted onto a wall or other surface.

Looter A person who steals from buildings during an emergency.

Magma Molten (melted) rock under the ground. When it spills onto the surface it is known as **lava**.

Mosaic A picture made from tiny cubes (**tesserae**) of coloured stone.

Nero Emperor of Rome, AD 54–68.

Paedagogus (pronounced **pee-da-go-gus** or **pie-da-go-gus**) A slave, often from Greece, who worked for a Roman family. His job was to take his master's son to and from school, and teach him how to be a good Roman citizen. The word means 'child guide' in Greek.

Philosopher A thinker or wise person.

Pumice A volcanic rock filled with air bubbles, making it very light in weight.

Refugee A person who has been forced to abandon their home.

Riot A wild disturbance by a crowd of people.

Scrinium A container for scrolls and writing implements.

Shrine A miniature temple where prayers can be offered to the gods.

Surge A sudden powerful movement in one direction.

Tablet A wooden board, covered with wax, used for writing on. Letters were scratched in the wax with a point called a **stylus**; the blunt end of the stylus was used to erase letters.

Tidal wave (or **tsunami**) A huge wave caused by an earthquake or eruption.

Titus Emperor of Rome, AD 79–81.

Tremor A small earthquake.

Villa A large house in the countryside.

Vineyard A place where grapes are grown.

Vulcan The Roman god of fire.

Index

Pliny, the Younger and the Elder

The Roman writer Pliny the Younger worked in government administration but is much better known to us today for his many personal letters describing private and public life at the height of the Roman Empire. He was an eyewitness to the eruption of Vesuvius in AD 79, because he was staying in his uncle's villa in the nearby town of Misenum. He described the event in great detail in a letter to the historian Tacitus.

His uncle, Pliny the Elder, met a nasty end at Stabiae, near Pompeii. The author of the famous *Natural History*, the world's first encyclopedia, Pliny the Elder was made commander of the Roman fleet at Misenum. When he spotted a strange cloud formation over Vesuvius, (which proved to be the volcanic eruption), he decided to go ashore to reassure the locals, but ended up suffocating in the deadly fumes. Volcanic eruptions of this kind are now called 'Plinian eruptions' in memory of this famous author.

Did you know?

Although many people have heard of Pompeii, its neighbour Herculaneum is much less famous, despite suffering the same fate in AD 79.

Herculaneum was a much wealthier town than Pompeii. Its residential quarter was filled with houses of the rich and middle class, opulently decorated with coloured marble, as well as many prosperous workshops.

When Vesuvius erupted, Herculaneum was also destroyed. Geologists believe that it might have been hit by a pyroclastic flow from the volcano. This is an avalanche of ash, rock fragments, and gas that rumbles down the side of a volcano, reaching speeds of over 100 kilometres per hour (60 miles per hour), and a temperature of more than 500 degrees Celsius (930 degrees Fahrenheit).

This extreme heat carbonized wooden and organic materials, like beds and food, in the town, preserving them for thousands of years in even better condition than the remains of Pompeii.

Although it was originally believed that all the occupants of Herculaneum managed to escape before it was engulfed by the volcano, excavation work that began in the 1980s eventually uncovered 300 people who seemingly fell victim to the deadly pyroclastic flow.

Top facts about Pompeii today

A Time Machine

Pompeii still fascinates people because it's one of the few places where the realities of daily life in the Roman Empire have been preserved. Visitors feel like they're stepping into a time machine and experience a sense of what it was really like to live as an ordinary person in Pompeii 2,000 years ago.

Tourist Destination

Pompeii is now one of Italy's most popular tourist destinations, attracting more than 2.5 million visitors every year. It was declared a UNESCO World Heritage Site in 1997, which means that it has been defined as a place of great historical importance and deserves to be protected from the effects of neglect, vandalism or destruction.

Employment in Pompeii

Many of the people who live in the area today make their living from the tourism and hospitality industries that have grown up around the famous town, working as tour guides, bus drivers, hotel staff and waiters.